Financially Fit Females

We Are Here, To Kick Your Financial Rear Into Gear!

National Directory
2013–2014

Welcome to the Financially Fit Females First Annual Member Directory!

I'm so excited to offer this Directory as part of your Member Benefits! Getting to know the other members of Financially Fit Females is part of the magic that lies within this group. We are all at different points in our Financial Journeys, but we are all working towards a brighter financial future for our families and ourselves. And—by joining Financially Fit Females—we have chosen not to do this alone.

It feels great to be supported, encouraged, and inspired by all of you and I hope you will continue to get to know your fellow members. We are all here to help one another kick our financial rears into gear!

You all continue to amaze me with the great progress you are making! Here's to a great year ahead of smart decisions, reduced debt, increased savings, and increased earnings, and here's to your financial success!

—Sharlene

Sharlene Douthit
Founder, Financially Fit Females
Sharlene@FinanciallyFitFemales.com
FinanciallyFitFemales.com

After a 20+ year career in corporate sales and marketing roles for Fortune 100 Consumer Packaged Goods companies, I took the leap and quickly became a serial entrepreneur, launching 5 companies in two years. Following my passions for photography, real estate investing and interior design. I created businesses that specialize in making things more beautiful, whether it is people, via my portrait photography, investment properties I renovate, or homes for sale that need some special professional home staging in order to sell fast, I have a natural ability to turn something average into something extraordinary. My pride and joy is Financially Fit Females. Created based on my own desire to become more financially savvy, this group's mission is to educate, encourage, and empower women to become financially fit by making the most of what they have, finding ways to earn more, spending and investing wisely, and passing their wealth and assets on to future generations.

A Very Special Thanks

Our success over the past year would not have been possible without the help of our catering sponsor, Ziva Chocolates. Julie Whitcomb and her talented staff have provided us with delicious, gluten-free appetizers at every Financially Fit Females meeting and catered lunches for the Financially Fit Females Mastermind groups. We encourage you to reach out to Ziva for all your chocolate and catering needs!

We would also like to thank the PPA Event Center for providing the space for our meetings and being so welcoming and easy to work with.

Kathy Anderson

Send Out Cards

www.sendoutcards.com/66581

sendcardswithkathy@yahoo.com

I am a Senior Distributor with Send Out Cards and my goal is to be your appreciation marketing consultant by making you, your products, and services unforgettable with greeting cards and gifts. The Mission Statement of Send Out Cards is to provide an avenue to act on your promptings by reaching out in kindness through greeting cards and gifts–– as well as provide a vehicle for financial freedom.

Adriane Anile

Grace in Gravity
adrianeanile@gmail.com

I graduated from the Rolf Institute® in Boulder, CO and I am also a registered nurse with a Bachelor of Science in Nursing. Several years ago, chronic back and neck pain due to injuries led me to try many healing modalities. Most of them were helpful but adding Rolfing Structural Integration is what enabled me to get out of my pain. Periodic maintenance sessions with a Rolfer and a consistent yoga practice help keep me pain-free.

My philosophy is one of empowerment. I do not work ON my clients, rather I work WITH my clients to help them achieve their goals of the session. My most important goal as a Rolfer is to seek the true potential of a client's body and facilitate them in achieving a pain-free and healthy lifestyle. I strive to find the body's innate ability to heal itself. I am passionate about sharing my knowledge, experience, and profound effects of Rolfing Structural Integration.

Renee Babkiewich

Reneebabkiewich.com
Renee.babkiewich@gmail.com

Nancy Buck

Edward Jones
www.edwardjones.com
nancy.buck@edwardjones.com

Originally from Cleveland, OH, I moved to Colorado in 2001 to bring family closer together. For fun, I horseback ride as much as possible, take my Miata out for spin with mom, gather with girlfriends for food and laughs, and go for long walks with my giant schnauzer.

I have been a Financial Advisor since 2001 and in the financial industry for over 30 years. I have passion for helping people achieve their financial goals with products that are well-suited for their specific situations, and for teaching as many young people as possible good saving and investing habits.

When it comes to your financial future, it's important to work with someone who takes time to understand you and your situation. We take a step-by-step approach to identify your goals and develop specific strategies to help you achieve them. Contact me today and see how personal service can make a difference.

Jennifer Burstein

Balanced Solutions, LLC
jennifer@balancedsolutions.biz
facebook.com/balancedsolutions.biz

As the owner of Balanced Solutions, LLC, I am passionate about fiscal health! After 15 years in nonprofit work, I started Balanced Solutions to help small and start-up businesses get their financial house in order so they can focus on their overall business goals and objectives. Specializing in QuickBooks, services include weekly, monthly, or quarterly fiscal administration including AP, AR, bank reconciliation, and financial report preparation. We also help clients with budgeting and creating systems to make day-to-day fiscal administration less time consuming. We also handle payroll and related taxes if needed. We work closely with our clients' CPAs to ensure accurate and timely tax preparation.

Jennifer Campbell

Legal Shield
jennscampbell.com
jenn@jennscampbell.com

Legal Shield gives you access to an attorney without the high hourly cost. For a flat monthly fee you can get advice from an attorney on unlimited issues. We also have the most comprehensive identity theft coverage available, including restoration by professionals. More services for your business.

Special Offer: $10 enrollment fee reimbursed for all FFF members!

Martha Carlin

Amazigh, Inc
mcarlin@amazigh-inc.com

I am a seasoned business executive with over 25 years of experience in real estate operations and management for large public company portfolios. I am the owner of Amazigh, Inc. a systems consulting business with expertise in Oracle Software implementations, real estate software solutions and big data analytics. In addition, I do operations consulting for multi-family asset owners and special servicers and receivers.

Trinity Clancy

Infinity Insurance Strategies
Perfectpolicytc@gmail.com
www.infinityhealthwise.com

I have a MA in education and have been an educator for more than 25 years. As an insurance broker since 2008, I am passionate about teaching people how to make the best decisions regarding their insurance.

• Health Insurance: The laws are changing and health insurance can be complicated. I represent numerous companies and can help you find the best insurance to match your financial goals.

• Home, auto and commercial insurance: I work with Wave Financial Partners to offer a one-stop shop with 38 companies for home, auto, and even commercial insurance. Clients often cut their premium costs and increase their coverage by shopping with us!

Leona Cohen

daveleona@msn.com

I am a Business Continuity Analyst at First Data. I specialize in helping business units prepare their response and recovery in the event of disaster.

Laurel Cunningham

laurelcunningham21@gmail.com

I am a full-time working mother of three active kids: Jordan (17), Mackenzie (14) and Alex (9). I live and work in beautiful Golden, Colorado. I earned my Bachelor of Science degree from Colorado State University.

As a Licensing Director specializing in brand building and procurement, I operated a bricks-and-mortar retail operation, mail order catalogs, e-commerce and mobile commerce websites, Business-to-Business wholesale program, warehouse, and fulfillment center, all of which included leading a team of 25+, running a P&L, sourcing and procuring merchandise, and working with brand teams on brand strategy and execution while generating revenue and turning a profit. I have 20 years of experience in leadership, strategy development and implementation, operating a business, brand building, sourcing and procuring merchandise, developing and launching websites, producing and mailing consumer catalogs, running a fulfillment center, and operating a business to business wholesale program while growing and generating bottom line profits to the organization. Hire me to deliver results through great leadership, brand building, and strategy execution.

Barbara de Jong

Edward Jones Investments
barbara.dejong@edwardjones.com
www.edwardjones.com

I opened a new office for Edward Jones in 2003, with goal of bringing convenient financial services to residents of Central Denver. Working closely with you and your CPA, attorney and other professionals, I can help determine the most appropriate financial strategy for you and your family, with special emphasis on creating a retirement savings strategy that will give you more options when you retire, regardless of what you decide to do. I am very active within my region of Edward Jones, having led the recruiting initiative to bring more women advisors to Edward Jones. I attained the CFP designation in spring 2013. I'm active in my neighborhood and community as well, serving on nonprofit and neighborhood boards, and volunteering at Denver Botanic Gardens. I also collaborated on a 550-page cookbook that was released in spring 2013.

Katie Edmiston

Independent Consultant, Arbonne International
kledmist@yahoo.com
www.arbonne.com

I am a "recovering auditor" who——after 10+ years in Corporate America——
decided to jump into my own business! Through Arbonne, I have found products
which produce results that are pure, safe, and beneficial in addition to being
vegan-certified and good for you! Not only have the products made a difference in
my life, but with Arbonne I have been able to enjoy the freedom that being an
entrepreneur offers of both time and financial freedom. More importantly this
has shown me and my team that it is possible to live the life of my dreams and I
am on her way to doing just that!

Special Offer: Free skincare, makeup, or nutrition consultation! Ask me for a
sample of our magic eraser for your skin! It truly helps get rid of all the things
you have trouble with and it's good for you.

Carol Engel-Enright

Internship Coordinator & Professor,
Department of Design and Merchandising
Colorado State University

Regional Director
Fashion Group International of Denver

Founding Board Member
Denver Design Incubator

Nathalia Fairbault

Birdie Belt
Style Therapist
www.styletherapist.com

I owned and operated seven Great Clips franchises for ten years before moving to Colorado in 2002. I sold my last franchise and started a fashion consulting business called Style Therapist. After starting to play golf, I decided to invent, design, and patent a women's golf accessory called Birdie Belt. It won Best New Product at the PGA show in Orlando in 2010! I am presently selling it directly out of my home and in golf shops around the country.

Diane Gaston

Morey Middle School, Denver Public School District | Diane_Gaston@dpsk12.org
Women Enjoying Beer - Colorado Representative |
Diane@WomenEnjoyingBeer.com | www.WomenEnjoyingBeer.com |
Tinkertown Designs, LLC – STEM Consulting, Lead Tinkering and Creative
Educator |TinkertownDesigns@gmail.com | www.TinkertownDesigns.com |
www.facebook/TinkertownDesigns | Twitter: TinkerDesigns |

I am a middle school Technology Education teacher. I have a Bachelors of Science
in Technology Education from the University of Wisconsin-Stout and a Masters
Degree in Integrating Technology in the Classroom from Walden University. I am
the recipient of several prestigious awards for teaching and for my volunteer
work with Leave No Trace, and I am deeply involved in education in Colorado.
My work as an educator has evolved into public speaking and consulting
opportunities with Tinkertown Designs. In my "free" time I explore the world of
beer through my work as the Colorado Representative for Women Enjoying Beer,
a beer education, marketing, research, and consulting company based in Oregon.
I have been living and teaching in Colorado since 2002 and enjoy backpacking,
downhill skiing, and going to concerts at Red Rocks.

Mary Gaul

The Gift of Time, LLC
TheGiftofTimeLLC.com
mary@thegiftoftimellc.com
facebook.com/TheGiftofTimeLLC

The Gift Of Time, LLC, a personal assistant service, is here to provide essential services to anyone juggling life's demands and commitments in their business and personal lives. Our goal is to give you back some time to connect with the people and things that bring you peace and happiness. We are here to get things off your to-do list!

Special Offer: Purchase a block of time for three hours or more and get one hour free!

Irene Glazer

Live Urban Real Estate
IreneGlazer.com
irene@ireneglazer.com

One's environment matters. A home is our refuge and central to everything we do and become. Finding people their special place that fits them, and betters their quality of life is extremely rewarding, and that is why I became a Realtor.
With exceptional market knowledge of Denver's classic neighborhoods and up-and-coming hot spots, the support of cutting-edge technology, and award-winning marketing, I'm dedicated to making your home-buying and selling experience about you. My philosophy is that knowledge, ethics, and plain hard work are key to earning your confidence and trust.
I'm "not a native, but I got here as fast as I could." I've lived and played in Colorado for quite a few years––let me show you what's great about our state. Whether you're buying or selling your first home or your next one, I'll help you live the life you want.

Debra Goodman

Goodman Group of Colorado
Dgoodman7@comcast.net
www.sendoutcards.com/realgoodcards

I believe life is a journey best lived with a strong community of relationships. The purpose of our business is to assist others in building stronger relationships with their family, friends, and clients by providing low-cost marketing and support services through the Send Out Cards system: Database updates, marketing solutions, business tools, referral systems, cards, and gifts at your fingertips.

Janiece Gurule

Trust the Curves, Speaking and Coaching
Gurul003@regis.edu

I am an inspirational, powerful, positive, and encouraging speaker who will touch your heart with spirit and passion. I am an expert in the dynamics of change and resilience. My work and life experiences support my ability to coach, lead workshops, and teach through public speaking. If you need an encouraging speaker, I am the lady who will bring you passion as well as touch your heart!

I received my MA in Communication and Psychology with Master certificates in Organizational Training and Development as well as Life/Career Coach from Regis University. I am certified in Mediation from Mountain States Employee Council. I have worked with organizations such as Junior Achievement, (JA in a Day and Business week), and The Conflict Center.

Special Offer: For our fabulous FFF members you will receive your first one-on-one private coaching session with me at no cost.

Jendayi Harris

Next Level Therapy, LLC
jharris@nextleveltherapy.com
www.nextleveltherapy.com

I am an Emotional Fitness Trainer, specializing in father wounds and dysfunctional upbringing effects, including struggles around depression, fear, weight, eating, self-esteem, anger, and forgiveness. I am the owner of Next Level Therapy which provides on-demand Christian counseling and transformational groups. Passionate about the mental, emotional, spiritual, and relational health of the community, I enjoy collaborating with organizations to provide programming and supportive conferences. I provide emotional strength training plans to individuals serious about overcoming negative cycles in their lives and growing in love, peace, and joy. I have a Masters in Counseling Psychology from Colorado Christian University, Business degree from Seton Hall University in NJ, and board certification with the American Association of Drugless Practitioners from the prestigious Institute for Integrative Nutrition in New York City.

Michelle Hartzell

Isagenix International
www.healthreward.com
www.losemymommytummy.com
www.facebook.com/myhealthreward

I provide solutions to transform lives and free people from physical and financial pain, as well as solutions for weight loss, energy and performance, healthy aging, and wealth creation. As a registered nurse with over 20 years of women's health experience, my passion is to help guide you towards improved health and wellness. Building a team that improves health and wealth is my dream come true!

Christina Johnson

Beacon Wellness Solutions

healthyliving123@wedeliverwellness.com

I am passionate about helping people take control of their health. I focus on providing education on the effects of toxins on our bodies and how to safely remove them from your home. I help my clients become better educated consumers which can help them save both money and time while shopping for better, safer products for themselves and the environment.

Special Offer: Free consultation and house cleanse (kitchen, bathroom, and laundry room)

Hanna Kubiak

Rodan + Fields

I was a successful international business development executive in aerospace, with a 16+ year management career of delivering revenue growth through strategic partnerships and operational excellence. A first-class communicator with a consultative selling style and strong negotiation skills, I am a passionate product evangelist in entrepreneurial settings. I'm also a keen problem solver with an exceptional aptitude for understanding colleague and customer needs across cultural and language barriers. I am multilingual, with business and travel experience in 40+ countries. Today, I follow my passion of mentoring by connecting entrepreneurs with the products, knowledge, resources and opportunities to change their skin, and their lives. I'm working in a $6 Billion US market with professionals from all backgrounds; teachers, nurses, real estate professionals, lawyers and CEOs, who are tired of long hours and salary caps or cuts, not enough time with their families, and job instability. They're now building businesses from home in part-time hours that create more money and greater flexibility, providing a lucrative income and better quality of life.

Patricia Langlois

Patricia Langlois, CPA, PC
www.DenverTaxDiva.com
patty@denvertaxdiva.com

I have been providing services as a CPA for 20 years. I specialize in income tax preparation, planning and bookkeeping, and accounting for small business owners, entrepreneurs, real estate brokers, investors, mortgage brokers, and network marketing professionals. I also provide payroll services and assistance with loan documents for borrowers, and CPA letters for loan underwriters that may be required to qualify for a loan. I assist taxpayers with IRS issues and in communicating with the IRS. My consulting services include real estate investment analysis, state and local income and sales tax preparation and compliance, and overseeing and developing work plans for accounting system clean-up projects and reconciliation projects.

Jeannine LeBrun

WITeee (Women In Transition: exploration, education, energy)
Jeannine109@comcast.net

I am a graduate of California State University–Chico, having earned a degree in Psychology with an emphasis in Career Life Planning. I have travelled extensively in Europe and Japan over the years and love to experience cultural diversity. I am a teacher, a writer, and a speaker, having worked with Campus Life/Youth for Christ, Intervarsity Christian Fellowship, and organizations in Japan. I continue to evolve and grow with life's opportunities for change. I am passionate about seeing others and myself embrace their gifts and talents and living a life filled with the knowledge that we are unique and gifted for joy and purpose. I support the belief that as women we have much to offer and it is my goal to inspire and encourage women of every age to aspire to their ideal self. I reside in Lakewood, Colorado and I am a proud mother of two bright young adults.

Jean Lesmeister

Babysitter's Training JEANius and Adult CPR Now

jean@babysittingclass-cprnow.com

If you are in a class that has smiles and chuckles intermingled with the important curriculum, you retain more. I am a gifted instructor of youth Babysitting Safety classes and Adult CPR/AED and First Aid classes. With 13 years of experience teaching health and safety, as well as teaching college theatre classes, my classes are interactive and energetic. The youth classes prepare them with first aid skills and they leave class with confidence and pride, and their certification card in hand. Whom will they need to give care to? The people you spend the most time with, statistics say–– your family, your friends, and your co-workers. Strangers, less likely––but you're ready, if need be. Be there for your people. Get trained. You'll be glad you did!

Diane Lopes

diane.lopes@mtnfinancial.com
http://mtnfinancial.com
www.CashFlowObjectives.com

At Cash Flow Objectives-Mountain Financial, I advocate the truth and positively impact lives. I educate and empower individuals, families, and business owners in order for them to reach their personal, professional, and financial goals. Bottom line, I specialize in practical money techniques. I teach you how to make money work smarter for you, by utilizing a two-pronged approach: debt elimination (if applicable) and tax-free retirement planning. I utilize non-traditional methods and strategies to help my clients maximize current revenue and retirement objectives. I use four basic principles when working with you: Increase your money supply; create more and better benefits; reduce the element of risk and future taxes; and accomplish all this without spending one more dime than you are already spending. Your economic situation is a matter of choice, not a matter of chance.

Megan Luna

Arbonne International
Megan.luna@meganluna.com
Meganluna.myarbonne.com

I show people how to look and feel their best with skincare, health, and wellness products that are pure, safe, and beneficial (and––if they want to––earn a six-figure income while working part time from home!)

Senaiet Mesgun

African Renaissance
senaietmesgun@gmail.com

I have worked for the past 7 years as an Executive Assistant for top Fortune 500 companies, most recently for Arrow Electronics located in the DTC area. In this role, I have provided support to high-level executives as well as overseen logistics and communications support for a staff of over 150. I have also gained valuable experience volunteering with the Colorado PeaceJam foundation, The Eritrean Community Center and the Colorado I Have A Dream Foundation. I developed a passion for the arts and community involvement growing up in Denver as a child to immigrant parents. My love of learning about different cultures and world affairs continued through college at the University of Colorado at Denver. After finishing my degree in International Studies, focusing on Sub-Saharan Africa, I furthered my studies internationally attending conferences in Berlin with the Institute for Cultural Diplomacy. I hope to help lead an effort to develop a community focused on creativity, sustainability, and education. In my spare time I love to work on creative projects and enjoy Colorado's beautiful scenery through hiking or biking.

Bethany Neumann

Modern Woodmen of America
www.modern-woodmen.org
Bethany.neumann@mwarp.org

I help people get their ducks in a row! I love working with families and businesses to help get them prepared before life throws them the inevitable curve ball. I'm an independent agent with Modern Woodman, a 130-year-old not-for-profit insurance agency. We believe in giving back to the community while improving the quality of life for our members. It's one of the main reasons I chose to work for them.

Special Offer: Comprehensive financial analysis and forecaster for FREE! (A $750.00 value) I've met so many amazing women through Financially Fit Females that I've been able to help and now I'd love to help you! If you would like to see how I can offer you amazing coverage for a price you and your family can afford, please take me up on my special offer. I look forward to connecting with you!

Amy Nichols

Amy Nichols Productions
Email: Amy@GetResultsWithImpact.com
Facebook: www.facebook.com/AmyNicholsProdxns
Linked In: www.linkedin.com/in/ANPrdxns
Other: www.youtube.com/OAmyCat

I am a freelance Visual Media Producer and visionary who excels at working with people and projects that are making a positive impact in the world. For more than a decade, I have created, edited, and managed various content and marketing media. I am skilled in video production, graphic design, and writing for the Web and print, with an emphasis on clear, direct communication.

I approach creative work intuitively with an eye for capturing the appropriate audience, making an impact, and delivering an immediate call to action. My work experience includes Internet marketing, teaching, publications management, and business administration. Though I'm a creative at heart, I also have a BS in Biology and a minor in Chemistry.

Leslie Lane Peabody

Ninjas in High Heels, Business Coach and Author
lesliepeabody@me.com
www.LeslieLanePeabody.com

I am the author of the forthcoming book *Lead Like a Muther – or is it Mother? Leadership Secrets for Women*. I am a business coach who can help you exponentially expand your business by expanding your dreams and adding systems to help you achieve your dreams quickly––and by making sure your business works even when you aren't! My coaching business is called Ninjas in High Heels to celebrate that as women, we all have ninja skills.

Special Offer: All FFF members will receive an exclusive Ninja Strategy Session to assess where their vision can grow, systems can be added, and income streams can be leveraged to more highly monetize your business.

Judy Pfeifer

Re/Max Momentum
Judy4homes.com
Judy.pfeifer@remax.net

I was voted as a Five-Star Real Estate Professional in 2013. I have been selling real estate for over 14 years. When I have personal time, I spend it with my husband Tony, son Adam, and dog Ralph.

Special Offer: All FFF members receive a $500 credit at closing.

Renee Quintana Nunez

Body by Vi
shakemerenee@bodybyvi.com

I started my first 90-day challenge in April of 2012 and in my first year I lost 35 pounds. It made a huge difference in my life and ever since then I've been motivated to help others achieve their health-related goals as well. I love helping others feel great about themselves.

Special Offer: When you join the Body by Vi Challenge, you will receive a 10-day meal plan in addition to personal coaching for the first month.

Katie Robinette

Robinette Acupuncture
RobinetteAcupunctureDenver.com
katie.acupuncture@gmail.com
facebook.com/RobinetteAcupunctureDenver

I am passionate about helping people feel strong, healthy, and balanced. I use a combination of acupuncture, topical and internal herbal medicine, myofascial release, and heat therapy to reduce and eliminate aches, pains, and illness. I believer in the power of food and herbs to heal, and follow the principles of eastern nutrition both in my own life, and as guidance for my patients. I also promote the use of Chinese medicine as a preventative medicine, and value its ability to help people feel their absolute best. My mission is to use the abundant healing resources provided to us by nature to help people safely heal themselves and their families. I strive to encourage others to take charge of their lives, and not be passive about their health care.

Special Offer: One free 20-minute stress-reduction treatment.

Karen Sherwood

The Women's Small Biz Network
The Prosperity Shift
Karen@wsbiznetwork.com
www.wsbiznetwork.com

I am a Human Design Business and Prosperity Coach and Founder of the Women's Small Biz Network. As an award-winning coach, trainer, and facilitator for 14+ years, I utilize my intuition, the power of Human Design and Sacred Money Archetypes, as well as my extensive knowledge. I help both executives and small business owners capitalize on their innate talents, overcome their money blocks, have confidence in making, and learn to use their career or business as a transformational tool for prosperity in service to themselves and humanity.

Special Offer: With the 45-Minute Money Breakthrough session for Financially Fit Female members you will gain a completely new perspective by understanding your Unique Human Design and Your Sacred Money Archetypes! Visit www.theprosperityshift.com/fff/ for more details and take advantage of the FFF special pricing.

Lauren Sweeley

Create Interior Design
www.create-interiordesign.com
laurensweeley@create-interiordesign.com

I am Lauren Sweeley and I own Create Interior Design. I am a professional who will help you create your dream home while making smart home improvement decisions. I specialize in residential design in Denver. I take your vision and create a reality.

Special Offer: First 3 hours of interior design consultations at 50% off!

Barb Tobias

Thrift Talk Diva, LLC
Email: barbatobias@thrifttalkdiva.com
Website: www.thrifttalkdiva.com
Facebook: www.facebook.com/ThriftTalkDiva
Twitter: twitter.com/ThriftDiva
LinkedIn: www.linkedin.com/in/barbtobias
Pinterest: pinterest.com/speakerbarb
Radio: www.blogtalkradio.com/thetrashtalkshow

I am Barb Tobias, America's "Thrift Talk" Diva, and an admitted thrift-aholic. As a veteran columnist, radio host and TV personality I've criss-crossed the nation in my search for fabulously frugal finds and amazing women who have a story to tell. I am a professional speaker, award-winning author, newspaper columnist, and inspiring business consultant who renovates businesses and lives by sticking my curious little nose into other people's "thrifty business." My talks are powerful and interspersed with energy and lively humor as is my inspirational book, *Tossed & Found*.

Dawn Todd

Wildly Successful Women

Lee Weisbard

Weisbard Dental
lweisbard@aol.com
www.weisbarddental.com

As a general dentist in DTC for over 25 years, we offer a full range of cosmetic, general and implant services to address most dental issues. This allows us to improve your health and smile based on a complete evaluation. Our holistic approach addresses both short and long term dental wellness.

Special Offer: In office teeth whitening for $399 (Normally $600) and take home bleach trays to keep your teeth white and bright.

Julie Whitcomb

Ziva Chocolates
Zivachocolates.com
juliew@zivachocolates.com

I am the Founder and CEO of Ziva Chocolates in Denver, CO. Our mission is to be the leading alcohol-/spirit-infused chocolate and gourmet specialty chocolates/ sweets company in the world. We are about receiving in abundance so that we can give back in abundance and make a difference in helping individuals, families, children, and countries in need.

Special Offer: Use the coupon code FFF10 and receive 10% off your order before tax and shipping.

Meka Ziemer

Meka Creative Enterprise, LLC
mekacreative.com
meka@mekacreative.com

A professed free spirit, I live with my husband, Jason, in Lakewood, Colorado with our puppies Luna and Pickles. I am a self-taught artist who first started creating magical pictures six years ago and decided to make it a business. I have an eclectic background including a Bachelor of Science in Psychology, several worldly adventures exploring animal behavior, as well as seven years' experience in corporate America. Photo art allows me to show the possibilities in people and in life. It is so easy to forget about the magic of life and the amazing facets we all have when we only look at the concrete reality around us. Photo art gives me a platform to express this using photographs, graphic design, and drawing. Photo art allows me to celebrate each individual for their own unique beauty and expression.

Special Offer: 15% off photo art products.

Additional Members

Tobi Brenner	tobi.brenner@comcast.net
Mary Carter	mrycrtr@aol.com
Joy Choo	joychoo@yahoo.com
Sheila Cole	miatia2@gmail.com
Sheila Graves	sgraves922@aol.com
Scottie Iverson	swandenver@qwestoffice.net
Mary Kansny	dinnersonme@msn.com
Carolyn King	glamazon154@gmail.com
Heather Kreider	heatherkreider@gmail.com
MollyBeth Lombard	mblombard@me.com
Storm McNab	smallfrymcnab@yahoo.com
Shelli Schilke	wysiwyg108@gmail.com

www.ingramcontent.com/pod-product-compliance
Lightning Source LLC
Chambersburg PA
CBHW080919290526
45795CB00007BA/2585